My Very First Look at
Clothes

Christiane Gunzi

CHANHASSEN, MINNESOTA · LONDON

Everyday clothes

vest

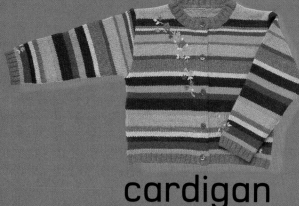

cardigan

shoes

pants

trainers

trousers

What clothes do you put on first?

My Very First Look at
Clothes

CHANHASSEN, MINNESOTA • LONDON

www.two-canpublishing.com

Published by Two-Can Publishing,
18705 Lake Drive East, Chanhassen, MN 55317

© Two-Can Publishing 2002

Conceived, designed and edited by

Picthall & Gunzi Ltd

21A Widmore Road, Bromley, Kent BR1 1RW

Original concept: Chez Picthall
Editor: Margaret Hynes
Designer: Paul Calver
Photography: Steve Gorton
Additional photographs: Daniel Pangbourne
DTP: Tony Cutting, Ray Bryant

'Two-Can' is a trademark of Two-Can Publishing.
Two-Can Publishing is a division of Creative Publishing international, Inc.
18705 Lake Drive East, Chanhassen, MN 55317.

ISBN 1–84301–084–4

2 4 6 8 10 9 7 5 3 1

A catalogue record for this book is available from the British Library.

Colour reproduction by Reed Digital
Printed in Hong Kong.

The publisher would like to thank the following people, companies and organizations
for their kind permission to reproduce their photographs:

Swatch (UK): 231

socks

shirt

knickers

jeans   skirt   pyjamas

How many trainers can you see?

Sunny days

T-shirt

straw hat

jelly shoes

visor

shorts

cap

sunglasses

Can you find the spotted pattern?

sandals

short-sleeved
shirt

sun hat

swimsuit

flip flops

sun dress

Point to the orange things!

Wet days

rain hat

raincoat

wellington boots

umbrella

waterproof trousers

What colour is the rain hat?

Cold days

jumper

trousers

woolly hat

gloves

scarf

puffa jacket

socks

boots

Point to the striped clothes!

Sports clothes

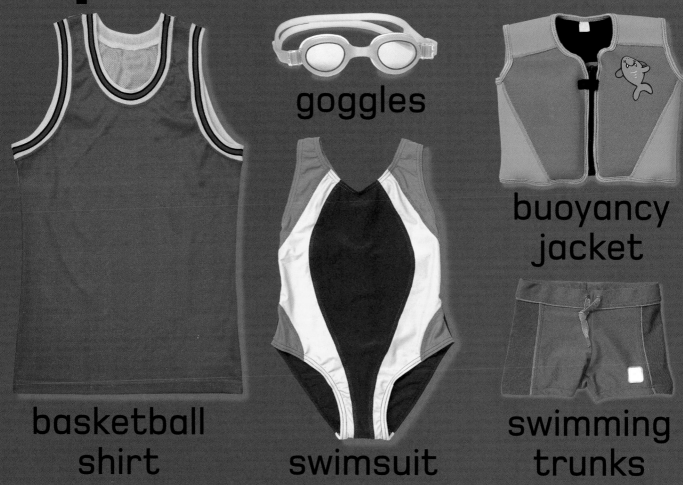

goggles

buoyancy
jacket

basketball
shirt

swimsuit

swimming
trunks

Can you find the goggles?

martial arts suit

football strip

Where is the green belt?

Work clothes

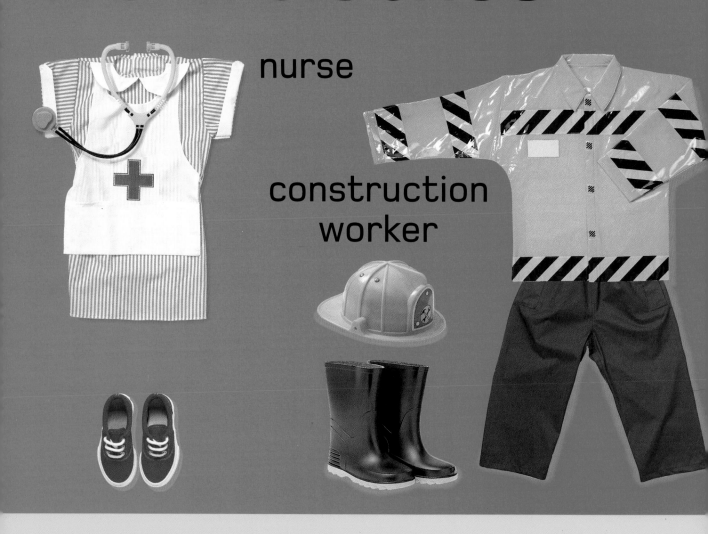

nurse

construction worker

How many boots are there?

chef

firefighter

Can you find the chef's hat?

Dressing up

pirate

wizard

Point to the starry robe!

fairy   mermaid   island girl

Find the pirate's hook!

At the ball

dinner
jacket

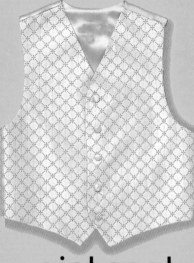

waistcoat

bow tie

braces

Where are the purple feathers?

tiara

feather boa

evening
gloves

evening
bag

shoes

ball
gown

What colour are the braces?

On my head

rain hat

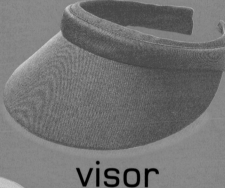

visor

party hat

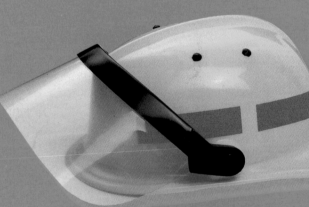

fire helmet

cycling helmet

Can you count all of these hats?

baseball cap

beret

woolly hat

riding hat

sun hat

Point to the diamond pattern!

On my feet

slippers

plimsoles

wellington boots

boots

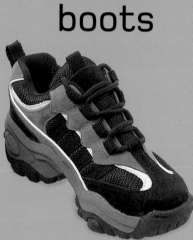

trainers

How many pairs can you see?

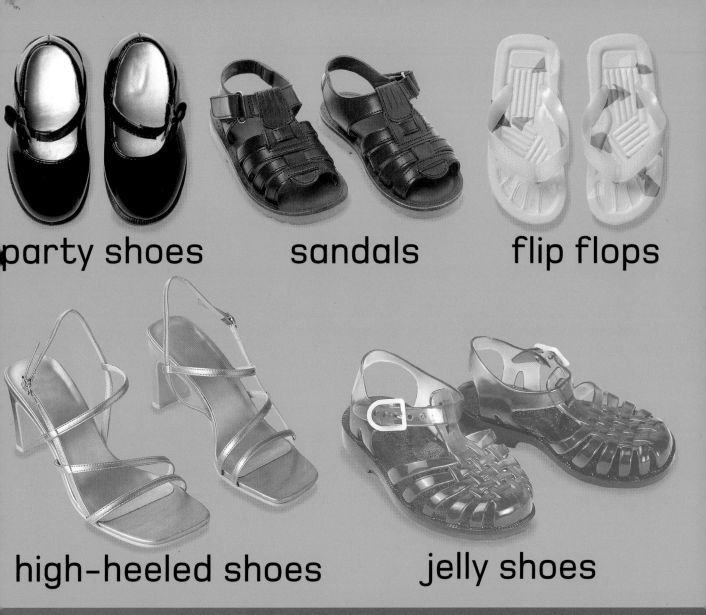

party shoes

sandals

flip flops

high-heeled shoes

jelly shoes

Find the buckles on the shoes!

Accessories

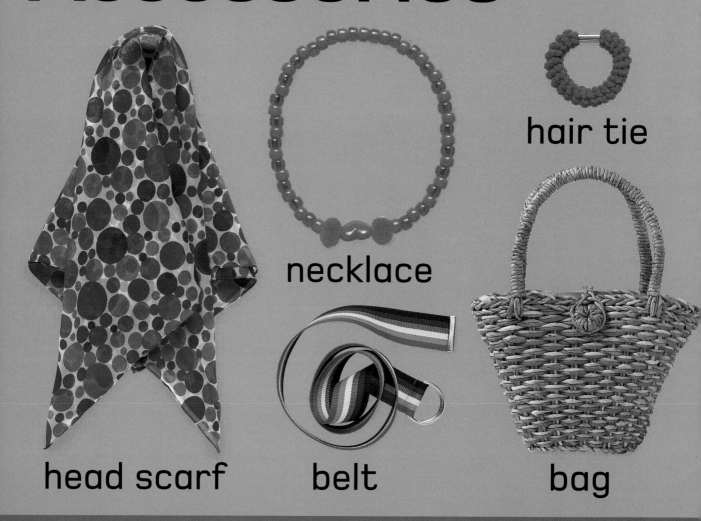

hair tie

necklace

head scarf

belt

bag

How many pink things can you see?

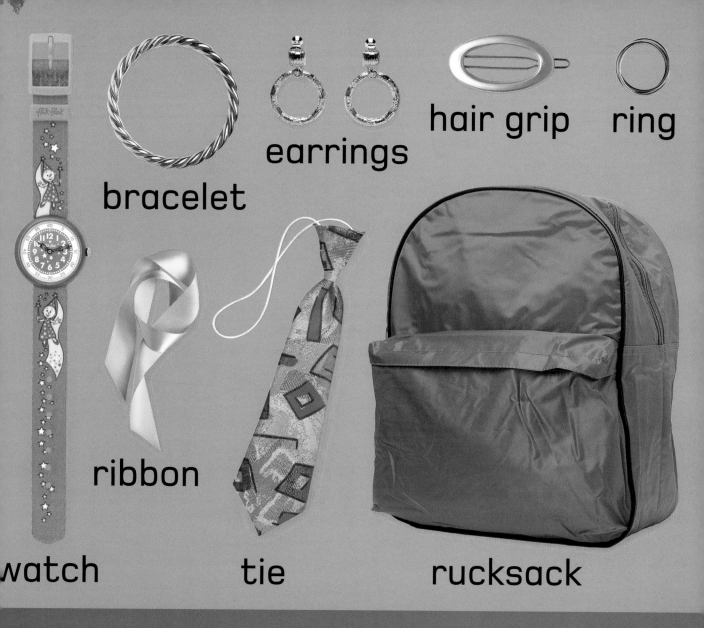

bracelet

earrings

hair grip

ring

ribbon

tie

watch

rucksack

What colour is the ribbon?

What do you wear?

woolly hat

trainers

scarf

slippers

bow tie

cap

Where do wear these things?